HOW CAN I EXPERIMENT WITH ... ?

A SCREW

David and Patricia Armentrout

Rourke

Publishing LLC
Vero Beach, Florida 32964

www.rourkepublishing.com

PHOTO CREDITS: ©James P. Rowan pgs 11, 27; ©David French Photography pgs 9, 13, 15, 19, 21, 29; ©Painet, Inc. pgs 17, 25; ©PictureQuest Cover, pgs 4, 7, 23.

Cover: *You can tighten or loosen a screw with a screwdriver.*

Editor: Frank Sloan

Cover design: Nicola Stratford

Series Consulting Editor: Henry Rasof, a former editor with Franklin Watts, has edited many science books for children and young adults.

Library of Congress Cataloging-in-Publication Data

Armentrout, David, 1962-
   How can I experiment with simple machines? A screw / David and Patricia Armentrout.
      p. cm.
Summary: Defines screws, explains their functions, and suggests simple experiments to demonstrate how they work.
Includes bibliographical references and index.
   ISBN 1-58952-336-9
   1. Screws--Juvenile literature. [1. Screws—Experiments. 2. Experiments.] I Title: Screw. II. Armentrout, Patricia, 1960- III. Title.
   TJ1338 .A758 2002
   621.8'82--dc21
                                                                    2002007765

Printed in the USA

W/W

Table of Contents

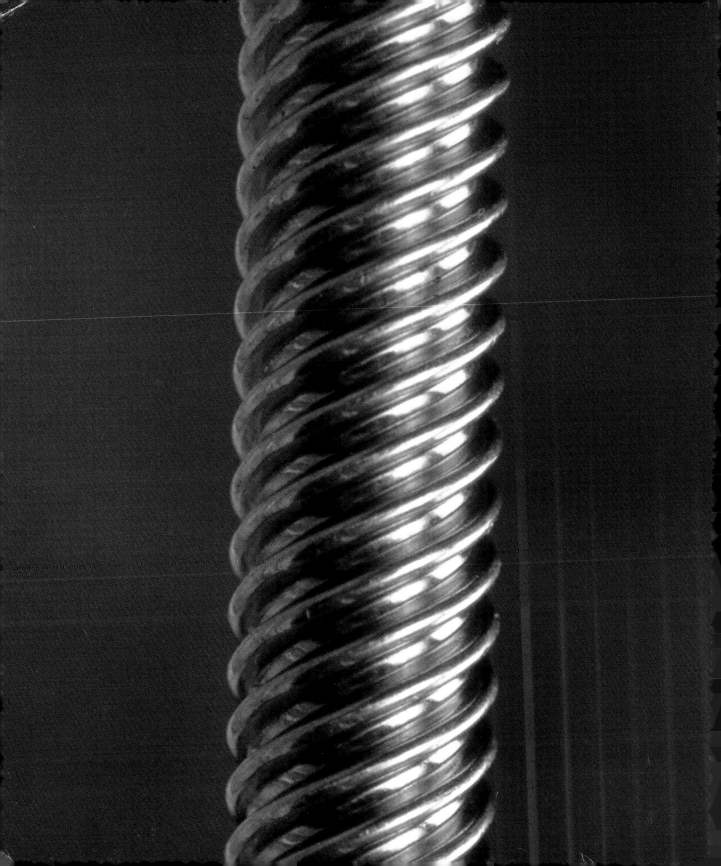

Screw (SKROO) — a flat sloping surface that winds around a shaft; a simple machine that makes work easier

A thread on a screw is a winding inclined plane.

Simple Machines

A good machine can do more, and work faster, than a person. Machines don't complain. Machines don't ask for raises. When a machine breaks, it can be fixed by people or other machines.

Do you know which machines were invented first? The answer is: simple machines. Simple machines are the wheel, the pulley, the wedge, the inclined plane, the lever, and the screw.

A power drill can make work faster and easier.

Tools

Simple machines made the lives of earlier people easier. Simple machines are tools. They were used to farm, to build shelters, and to make weapons and other tools.

You don't have to go far to find simple machines today. In fact, if you have a toolbox, that is a great place to start.

Do you have a hammer? A hammer is a lever. Even the nail you drive with a hammer is a simple machine. Nails are wedges. How about screws? Screws are simple machines, too. Most simple machines have one thing in common—they give us a **mechanical advantage**. In other words, they make our work easier.

Simple machines, like screws, wedges, and levers, can be found in a household toolbox.

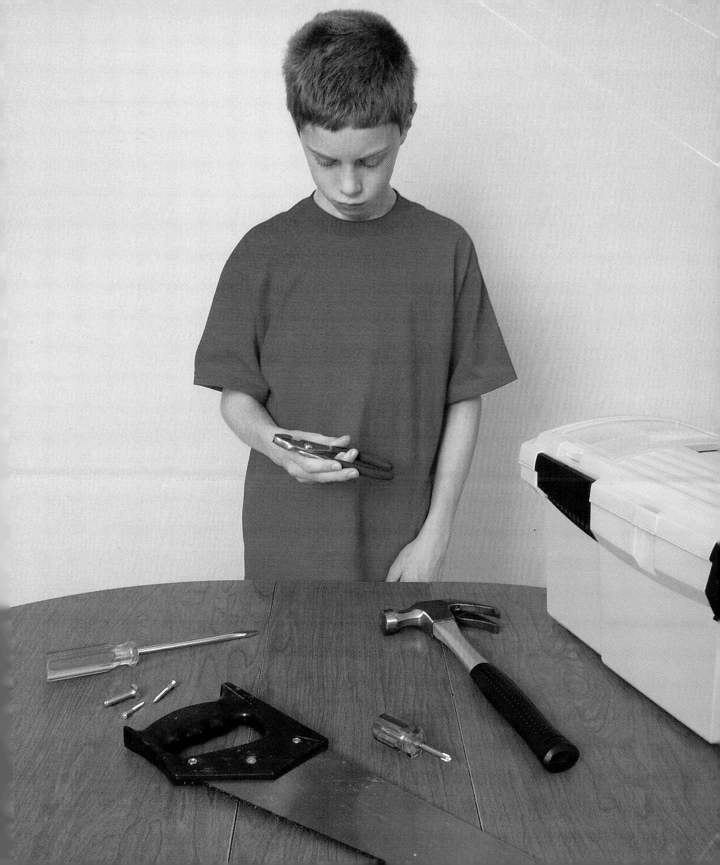

The Screw

A screw is a type of **inclined plane**. An inclined plane is a flat sloping surface. A screw is an inclined plane that winds around a shaft.

There are different types of screws, but most screws have a head, a shaft, and a tip. The shaft has a sharp ridge called a thread. The thread is an inclined plane that winds around the shaft. If you were to follow the thread from the tip, it would lead you to the top, or head, of the screw.

Screws are simple machines that allow you to apply a great amount of force with very little effort.

Most screws have a head, shaft, and tip.

Make an Inclined Plane

You will need:

- scissors
- plain piece of paper 6 inches square (15cm)
- color marker
- pencil

Use the scissors to carefully cut the paper diagonally. You should have two triangles. Discard one. With the marker, color a line along the edge you just cut. With the pencil, label one of the other sides "bottom." Hold the "bottom" edge over the table. The colored edge is an inclined plane—a flat sloping surface. Now, turn an inclined plane into a screw. Use the paper triangle for the next experiment.

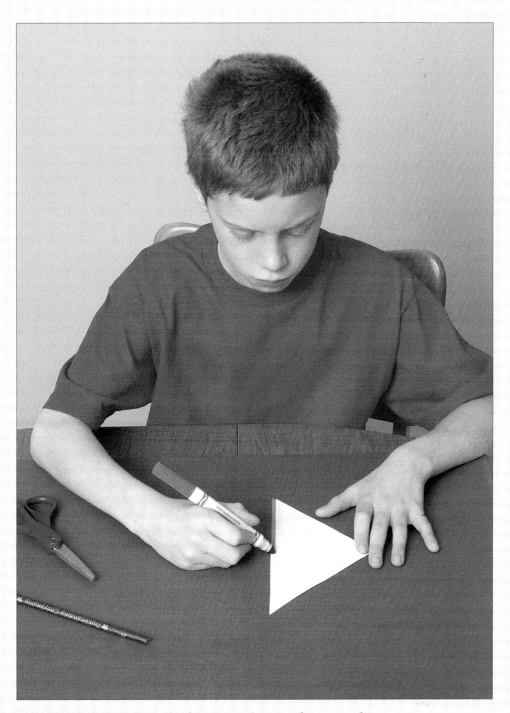

Mark your inclined plane with a color marker.

13

Make a Screw from an Inclined Plane

Place the paper triangle you just made colored-side down on a table. Place the pencil on one of the short sides of the triangle. Roll the pencil so the paper wraps tightly around it. Stand the pencil up. You should end up with a thread (colored edge) that twists up the shaft (pencil) of the screw. Is it easier now to see how a screw is a type of inclined plane?

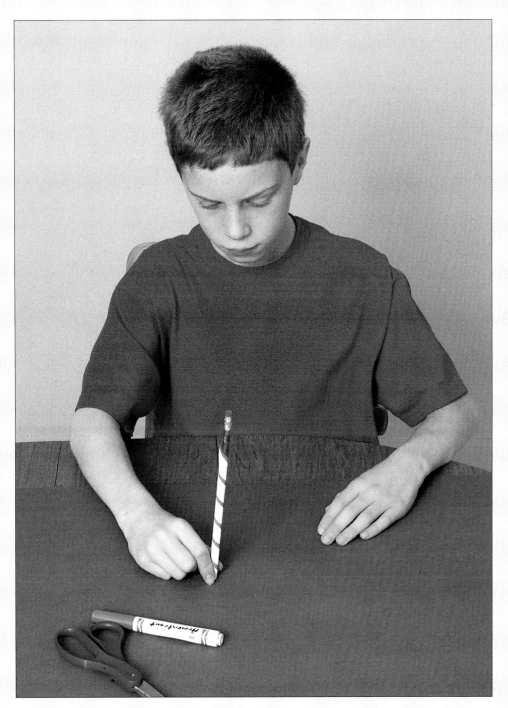

Your inclined plane is now a screw.

15

Screws That Hold

The main purpose of a screw is to fasten two or more materials together. Let's say you are working with wood, for example. As the screw is turned with a screwdriver, the tip will poke a small hole into the wood. Now the thread takes over.

The sharp thread cuts a spiral-shaped groove in the wood. The groove holds the screw tightly in place. When the screw passes from one piece of wood to the next, it holds the pieces together. If the screw is turned in the opposite direction, it can easily be removed.

The sharp thread on a screw cuts a groove into wood.

Using a Screw to Join Wood

You will need:

- 2 thin pieces of soft wood
- adult helper
- power drill
- a screw long enough to pass through 2 pieces of wood
- screwdriver

Place one piece of the wood on top of the other. Have the adult helper use the power drill to make a small pilot hole through both pieces of wood. Set the tip of the screw in the pilot hole of the top piece of wood.

Using your screwdriver, carefully turn the screw clockwise. You will need to apply some pressure. Keep turning until the screw has passed from one piece into the next. Once the screw has been tightened, try to pull the two pieces of wood apart.

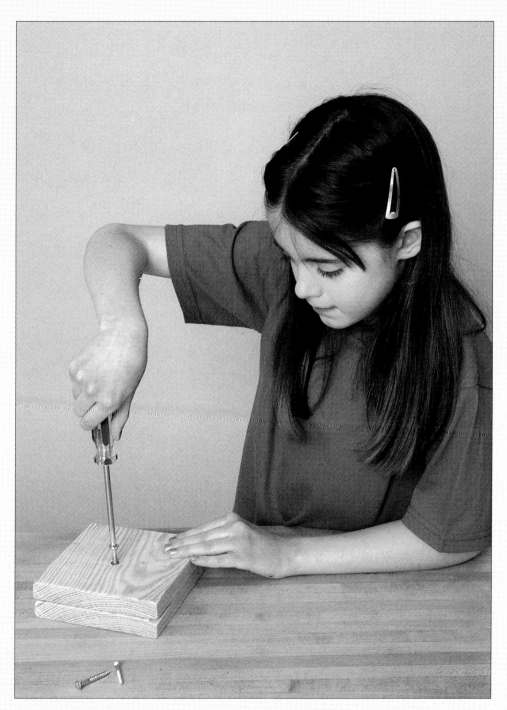

A screw can join two or more materials together.

Experiment with Different Kinds of Screws

The length of a screw's thread can make it easier, or harder, to turn. A short steep thread takes fewer turns, but more effort, to screw in. A long gradual thread goes in easier, but takes more turns to screw in. See for yourself.

You will need:

- adult helper
- power drill
- piece of soft wood
- masking tape
- screwdriver
- 2 screws the same size with different length threads

Have your adult helper drill two small pilot holes in the wood. Place a piece of tape on the handle of the screwdriver. Using the screwdriver, turn the first screw into a pilot hole. Watch the piece of tape and count the number of turns it makes as you drive the screw all the way in. Turn the other screw into the second pilot hole. Which screw was easier to turn?

It takes less effort to turn a screw that has a tightly wound thread.

Screws That Seal

Can you think of a screw that does not bore a hole? How about the lid on a jar? Take the lid off a jar of peanut butter. Look at the grooves on the inside of the lid. Now look at the thread on the rim of the jar. Notice how the grooves on the lid match the thread on the jar.

As you screw on the lid, the thread on the jar pulls the lid down until it forms a tight seal. The screw works so well that it would be nearly impossible to remove the lid without unscrewing it.

You are using a simple machine when you open or close the lid of a jar.

Screws That Dig

One useful type of screw is a drill bit. Drill bits are used to bore holes. Drill bits are also called **augers**.

A machine is used to spin a drill bit. As the drill bit spins, it cuts a hole. Material that has been cut moves up the drill bit's spiraling thread and out of the hole.

Drill bits come in all sizes. Some drill bits fit hand-held drills. Hand-held drills can quickly cut through wood and metal. Giant drill bits bore holes deep into the earth. They are used to dig for oil and for digging underground tunnels.

Drilling machines use giant screws to cut deep holes into the earth.

Screws on the Move

People have found many ways to use screws. Screws hold things together, seal containers, and **bore** holes. Screws can also propel, or push, boats through the water and airplanes across the skies.

A motor on a boat turns the propeller very fast. As it turns, the propeller pushes a stream of water behind it. The stream of water helps to propel the boat forward.

A motorboat's propeller works like a screw.

Experiment with a Propeller

Do you have any screws around the house that work like a propeller? How about a fan? Fans are propellers that turn much slower than the propeller on a boat or airplane.
Try this experiment:

You will need:

- balloon
- box fan

Fill the balloon with air and tie it off. Place the balloon on the floor 1 foot (30 cm) in front of the fan. Turn the fan on. As the fan's propeller picks up speed, what happens?

Turn the fan off. Now, place the balloon 1 foot (30 cm) behind the fan. Turn the fan on. What happens? You can't see the air, but you can see how the fan's propeller pulls air in and then pushes it out the other side.

A fan's propeller pulls air from behind and pushes it out the other side.

Glossary

augers (AW gerz) — tools used for boring

bore (BOR) — to make a hole with a tool that rotates

inclined plane (IN klynd PLAYN) — a flat sloping surface like a ramp or hill

mechanical advantage (mi KAN eh kul ad VAN tij) — what you gain when a simple machine allows you to use less effort

Further Reading

Macaulay, David. *The New Way Things Work.*
  Houghton Mifflin Company, 1998
Royston, Angela. *Screws.*
  Heinemann Library, 2001
VanCleave, Janice. *Machines.* John Wiley &
  Sons, Inc., 1993

Websites to Visit

http://www.kidskonnect.com/SimpleMachines/
  SimpleMachinesHome.html
http://www.most.org/sin/Leonardo/
  InventorsToolbox.html
http://www.brainpop.com/tech/simplemachines/

Index

About the Authors

David and Patricia Armentrout have written many nonfiction books for young readers. They specialize in science and social studies topics. They have had several books published for primary school reading. The Armentrouts live in Cincinnati, Ohio, with their two children.